FROM
RAGS TO
COMFORT

AN AUTOBIOGRAPHY

James Smith

authorHOUSE®

AuthorHouse™
1663 Liberty Drive
Bloomington, IN 47403
www.authorhouse.com
Phone: 1 (800) 839-8640

Published by AuthorHouse 03/20/2019

ISBN: 978-1-7283-0515-8 (sc)
ISBN: 978-1-7283-0514-1 (e)

Print information available on the last page.

This book is printed on acid-free paper.

My oldest memory is being in the back seat of a car when I was about two years old. I was sleeping and suddenly awoke to the car moving. I saw that the driver was an unknown individual who, I guess, was taking me and the car for a joy ride. After the driver noticed me, he immediately returned the car to where he found it and left the scene. I guess I was very lucky by today's standards. But things were so much more benign in those days.

I was born late in the fall of 1941 in a suburb of New York City. I was the youngest of three children. My brother was seven years older and my sister four years older than me. My brother and I were not particularly close due to the age difference. He had a very oppositional personality and took his frustrations out on me. I was closer to my sister mostly because of our brother's unpredictable behavior.

My mother was a cute little lady of Jewish decent whose family emigrated from Russia. She was born in Chicago. I remember her as a very sweet lady with a heart of gold.

My father was a Scottish immigrant from Edinburgh whose family settled in New York. He became a building superintendent, so we moved frequently around the city, in several areas of New York City. My father was pretty sick most of my young life. He was in and out of the hospital, suffering from liver and stomach disease. These days it would probably be diagnosed as cancer. We could play tic-tac-toe on his stomach from all of the operations he had.

My father was a stern man who took control of things. It became hard for my father to maintain his superintendent duties during his illness, so the union sent him a helper. I was playing outside when I got the news that my dad had passed away. He was fifty-six, and I was fourteen.

The man who had been his helper—I will call him Joe—stayed on. He was a big, burly man, about six feet, two inches tall and weighing over two hundred pounds. I often helped him with routine duties, such as dealing with the trash. In those days, New York buildings had incinerators. My job was to shovel the garbage into the incinerator and roll the trash cans, hand over hand, to the outside courtyard. Then I had to attach a metal gadget with two hooks on either side, go up the stairs, and use a pulley to get the cans back to the street, about thirty feet.

I found out later that Joe had been a professional fighter somewhere in New Jersey (I think). He gave me a pocket watch, which was engraved with his champion status. His hands were very large, and his nose had been broken several times. He also had fighter's ears, sometimes called "cauliflower ears." He had done many jobs, including longshoreman and short-order cook.

Eventually, my mother and Joe got married, and he became my stepfather. I actually remember a time when my father was sick, and I swear that I caught Joe kissing my mom. When asked, my mom said she was whispering something to Joe. He and I became good friends. He ran a tight ship, which my brother didn't like. Soon after, my brother joined the navy. He was seventeen.

My brother had a very bad temper. He and my father fought a lot. One time they got into it at the dinner table, and it got so bad that my mother called the police. Another time my father went after him with a wooden bed slat.

When my brother went into the service, my mother found a drawer full of parking tickets in his bedroom. One day the police came to the door and arrested my mother because the tickets had gone to warrant. The judge asked my mother what business she had owning this car. She answered, "That is none of your affair." The judge held her in contempt, and she was escorted to jail. There she was strip-searched like a common criminal. She spent her hours in jail contemplating how she was going to kill my brother. Eventually, she paid a heavy fine and was released.

My brother was very hard to control. He thought he knew it all. Once he bought a car and decided to take me and my sister for a ride. We didn't know he had no license. He went down Park Avenue in the wrong direction. At the end of the street was a police car, which my brother hit. This fiasco cost my parents a bundle. In those days, almost anything could be solved with enough money.

Seasons in the East were so definite and distinct that I always looked forward to them. At age five, I was sick for a very long time. I had a mastoid infection that could not be cured. These were the days before penicillin. I finally had to be hospitalized, and they operated to remove the mastoid bone behind my right ear. During my post-op recovery days, I made key chains and potholders. I guess the hospital had a crafts program for their pediatric patients. I went to a room on the top floor of the hospital to do these crafts. To this day, I have to be careful during cold, windy weather to protect my ear from infection.

Other childhood memories include wanting to play the drums. I wanted a drum set so badly, but I never got one.

One time while playing in the street, I found a dead baby. I fortunately don't remember much about this.

I attended the local public school, which was about five blocks from our building. In New York, the schools were all named PS and some number. I was so impressed with the white strap and badge of the safety patrol members. I wanted to be one of them. You had to be an A or B student to do this. Finally I was admitted into the group and wore my strap and badge proudly. I was so excited to have been chosen. Other school memories include buying my little milk carton each day and reading the *New York Times* during class and discussing current events. One day I got into a fight with a kid about something. I went home crying and told my dad. Not much was done as he was so busy working that he didn't have time to address the issue.

As I got older, I played stickball. We took new or used brooms and removed the head. We used the stick part to hit the pink rubber ball made by Spaulding. This game was very popular in my neighborhood.

On Saturdays, my sister and I went downtown to go roller-skating at a rink. We had to take the subway and carry our skates in little square boxes. The boxes came in a variety of colors and looked like large chrome camera cases. We met our friends at the rink. My sister had a special friend named Olaf, and they seemed to get along fine. He may have been her first boyfriend. When we skated to the song "zana, zana," we associated it with him.

After sixth grade, I went to the neighborhood middle school. By that time, we had moved to another building. Being older, I got to help with some of the jobs around the building. I even served as doorman. It was during this time that I began to smoke. My mother smoked Pall Mall Reds, and I think my father smoked Chesterfields. I smoked Lucky Strike.

When I was thirteen, I got a job in an arcade in Times Square, winding the toys in a window display. I thought I was such a big shot getting fifty cents an hour to do this. I had to take the A train to get to work. We also had to have "working papers" to get hired. I had to ride the subway downtown to get my papers approved for the job. I liked earning my own money and looked forward to the work.

During my teens, I continued to find ways to earn money, which I saved and put toward my social life. One time I went to a party at my girlfriend's house near Yankee Stadium with a couple friends. During the party, we met a girl who was there alone. She lived somewhere in the upper Bronx. She wanted to go home, and thinking it was not safe for her to go home alone at that hour, my friends and I offered to go with her. When we arrived at her house, we found out that her boyfriend was the leader of a large street gang. When we left, we found two guys sitting on her steps waiting for us. They physically detained us, and I had to do some fast talking.

Finally, the girl's boyfriend came along with several more reinforcements. We were in big trouble. I told him that I was protecting his girlfriend by escorting her home, and he should be thanking us. One of the gang members pulled out his switchblade to scare us. I kept assuring the leader that we were no threat to him. Finally, he must have believed us because he became friendlier toward us. He even offered to give us protection in our neighborhood. They escorted us to the subway and sent us home. We let out huge sighs of relief. They actually did come to our neighborhood to make sure that we had told them the truth about where we lived and to make sure we were no threat to them.

Finally it was time to decide which high school to attend. In those days you could either pick college prep or academic school or you could go to a vocational high school. I had been working on Saturdays for a company which made radios and I decided that I enjoyed learning about electronics. Besides I was enthralled with the service man's carrying caddy and the tubes. The only school in the New

York system for this kind of training was in Brooklyn. So I traveled on the A train every day to get to school. It took approximately an hour and a half to get there and then a five block walk. I had to leave my house by 7:00 to arrive for a 9:00 start.

The highlight of my day was playing hand ball every lunch hour. I had my main coarse classes, (TV service) for three hours each day and the rest of the time we had academics like math, English and history. My mother worked nights so I was alone in the evenings with my homework. My school was very racially integrated. I was one of the few white students and it was all boys. But everyone seemed to get along and mind their own business.

I never had a desire to go on to college. In those days many kids just went to work. After graduating we moved again but back to the suburbs. My mother was remarried to a man who was the produce manager of our local supermarket. The thing I remember about this step-father was that he loved my mother and he was very cheap. They stayed married about a year and then had the marriage annulled.

It was while living in the suburbs that I met my first serious girlfriend. She lived next door to me and her father was a bookie of some sort. I took her to her high school prom. We really got along well but she had her sight set on college.

After her graduation she went off to a university. I visited her occasionally but it became apparent that we were growing apart. We lost track of one another for a long time but I managed to find her in the 1980's. She was married and a college professor.

My first job was working for a company that made and repaired phonographs. I was called an electronic technician. It was my job to check the phonographs as they came off the line for the correct readings and functions. This job paid $60.00 a week. I worked there for about six months. I began to get bored. I remember taking my lunch with me every day and eating it in my car. I had bought a 1955 Turquoise Ford from my Uncle.

This reminds me of an incident with another car I once bought. It was a Pontiac Star Chief. My uncle and I were on or way to the bowling alley when the car stalled at a stop sign. Someone had told me once that you should check for a spark when this happens. I touched the ignition wire to the carburetor and when I did the car caught on fire. I ran to the trunk to grab the bowling balls and my uncle and I stood on the sidewalk and watched the car burn. The horn for the volunteer fire department blew and the fire fighters finally came. I tried to blend in with the crowd that had gathered to watch. When the fire fighters asked whose car it was I kept my mouth shut. The car was totaled. They put that high pressure hose under the hood to extinguish the flames and that was the end of the car.

My uncle was my friend and played a big role in my life. He was a confirmed bachelor and worked for the US post Office. He was a supervisor there for over 30 years and retired with a full pension. He was my mother's brother and we got along famously. He was a world pistol champion with many trophies to his credit. I still have some of his ribbons and trophies. He also made his own fishing rods and tackle. He was a man's man and I admired him very much. I can remember that he smoked Camel cigarettes. Those were unfiltered and strong. Bowling was one of the interests which we had in common. I would practice every chance I got. I became fairly good in this sport and jointed a few leagues. I ended up bowling almost every night. After the league games they would have "pot games". In those games you would bowl one on one for so much money per game (10 to 100 per game). I did pretty well at these. My average was in the low 200's at that time. My uncle and I would travel around to different alleys to see if we could win their 250 trophy.

I remember traveling to Dover, Delaware to see the largest bowling alley around. They had 100 lanes in a row. What a sight.

I next took a job with a company that serviced radios and TV's. I remember that the owner was an MIT graduate. One day they sent me on a call to Harlem. I went to the building and took my life in my hands. After taking the back off the TV set, out came hundreds of roaches. Needless to say this job didn't last long. I quit after a week. There had to be something better.

My next job was with a company called Panorama. There I took the schematic plans for making the wire lengths for particular projects and ran a cutting machine to cut the wires to prescribed lengths. I had one female employee under me. I was only 18 or 19 and had never managed anyone before. She did the "tinning "in a big vat of solder. Again I got bored with the job and would find ways to keep it interesting. Sometimes I would say that the machine was broken so they would send me out to find the broken part. This job had nothing to do with radio or TV repair so I pursued another TV company near Scarsdale, NY.

I started at $90.00 a week which was big money in those days. My co-worker became a good friend. We spent a lot of time together and I eventually moved into his house where he lived with his father also know as Pop. Pop was Italian and made a mean spaghetti sauce the old fashioned way. He used just butter and garlic.

I later stayed at the local YMCA. The rooms were comfortable except for the friendly creatures which occasionally scampered across the floor. The rooms were about 8x10 and there was a shared bathroom down the hall. I paid $8.00 to $10.00 a night. It served its purpose.

While staying there I met a very beautiful girl at the local lunch cafe. She was about 5'9" with beautiful long blond hair and a milky complexion. She worked at the neighborhood travel agency. We dated for a while and eventually fell in love. I knew I needed a better job so I interviewed with a local appliance company in Mt Vernon, NY. I got hired to do TV servicing and installation of appliances. I enjoyed the job because it provided a variety of experiences. I would install TV antennas on two and three story houses with steep slate roofs. I also delivered refrigerators up many flights of stairs. I had to carry the appliance on my back. Before I could put the new one in place I had to remove the old one, also on my back and down the stairs. I loved meeting the customers and visiting with them as I worked. The store owner recognized my skill at sales and he allowed me to go home after my shift, change clothes, and return to help on the sales floor. I found that I knew a lot about the appliances, inside and out because of my service experience. Within a short time I was outselling the other salesmen. I even gave the owner a run for his money. I really respected the owner an learned a lot from him. I wanted to work full time as a salesman but they did not any vacancies. They were about to open another store in a nearby town and said I could start my sales career there. I was excited at the prospect. My relationship with my girlfriend was getting more intense and we finally set a wedding date for September 30, 1962.

I worked long hours helping get the store ready for its opening. We brought in inventory and arranged things to the owner's liking. After all of the hours of work, I still did not have a permanent commitment to a permanent sales job. They still thought of me as a service man. I began looking in the papers for another job. I found an ad with a competitor's store in Yonkers.

I went for an interview and met with the owner. He was Italian and reminded me of a Mafia character. The owner seemed to really like me and he offered me the salesman job which paid $180.00 a week plus commission. This was exciting to me especially since I was newly married.

I did very well there. I ended up taking a lot of my former company's business. My former store didn't realize how good I was until I worked for their competitor. As time went on I found working at this store difficult because of the owner. He was a bit of con man and told everyone what they wanted to hear, not what they needed to hear. He also was a big gambler and was in trouble with his bookie. The atmosphere wasn't the best for me so when my former boss asked me to return in a sales position I left. This time he offered me a manager position and a salary of $225. a week plus commission. I was on top of the world!

We were quite a sales team. One guy whose name was Jack was a good tennis player. Another salesman called Manny was a heavy cigar smoker. Both guys were at least 20 years older than I. I am sure that there must have been some animosity between us as I always outsold them both.

Sarah and I got married as planned. We had a Catholic ceremony in her home church. Since I wasn't Catholic, we couldn't get married on the altar, but on the floor in front. Regardless, the ceremony was legal both for the church and the state. We went to Puerto Rico for our honeymoon and then resided in small, studio apartment near my work. Susie continued to work for the travel agency and soon became pregnant. After giving birth to our daughter, she quit the job to be a full time mom. By that time we had moved into a small house owned by a friend of my uncle. We soon moved to an apartment in Yonkers close to the appliance store. I remember that it was on the second floor. It had two bedrooms and was in a pretty nice neighborhood. I remember ordering a set of encyclopedias from a door to door salesman and then cancelling the order soon after. One of the baby items I remember buying was a "stroller chair". It was a piece with many functions from stroller, to high chair to toddler chair. I still have a picture of our daughter sitting in the chair taken in this apartment.

It was always my goal to own my own house. The American dream! My family had no extra money to share. In fact we had been on welfare at times to make ends meet. My mother was in New York at the time, my brother stationed in Italy and my sister was living in Chicago so I knew I was on my own. So, I set my sights on being a homeowner. I worked many hours trying to save enough for a down payment. I finally found a small house about 50 miles away from my work on an acre of land and It was in my price range. The house was blue and the living room was so small that only a couch would fit. I felt so proud of myself for accomplishing this goal at such a young age. My mother gave me a car to go back and forth to work. It was a Hillman Minx. It was small and had a stick shift but it was a great help. I really felt that my life was beginning to come together.

I commuted an hour each way to work and I was working six days a week, ten hours a day. Usually everyone was asleep when I got home although Susie sometimes stayed up so we could talk. I spent my day off at home enjoying the yard and playing with my daughter. I can still see her playing in the sandbox. I remember that I wanted to barbeque but it was winter and the snow was falling. I barbequed right in the entry doorway on the tile. I cracked the tile. I remember that when we moved it was winter and the oil burner was almost empty. I had spent everything I had to get into the house so I made arrangements for the oil company to bill us so we could get a delivery. Buying on credit was not as common in those days. Soon after settling into our house, Susie announced she was pregnant.

Our son was born the following December. Things went along well for a while. I worked and Sarah mothered our kids. By and by I began to notice some changes at home. Sometimes I would find my wife passed out when I got home. I found that she had begun drinking. It got so bad that I had to teach my three year old daughter to call me at work when she found mommy on the floor. It got progressively worse and the calls from my daughter were more frequent.

One night I got a call and left work to head home. When I got there I found another man in the house. They had both been drinking heavily and he left without incident when confronted. I didn't know what to do. I needed to work and had no one to help with the kids. It was surprising that I held on to my job through all of this but my boss quite understood. I decided that I needed to sell the house and move closer to my work. The house I had paid $18,000 for had to be sold for $16,000. We moved into an apartment until we could find something bigger.

We took a short vacation to Canada and while there Sarah had a seizure. I later found out that she had had an epileptic seizure. Apparently this was caused by her withdrawal from alcohol.

Her mother and I finally convinced her to admit herself into a hospital for alcohol rehab. Now the problem was who would take care of the children. Child Social Services offered to provide someone to watch the kids while I worked. This continued for six months. But my wife's treatment was for a year.

My daughter started her first day of kindergarten during this time. I remember taking her to her first day and thinking that her mother should be there with us. The whole situation was very sad. The kids did not deserve this.

My son was watched by a caseworker most of the time so I could work. This time in his life affected him a lot. He cried for his mommy and he didn't understand where his mother had gone. I did my best to be both parents to the kids but it was difficult for me being so young myself and having to be gone from them for work. None of us deserved what we got. We didn't have too many options. Neither family was really around for support, no close friends in a position to help, and little money. Every decision was on me.

When the year had passed and my wife was ready to come home, she announced that she wasn't coming home to me and the kids. By this time I had exhausted all of my options through the social services. I have to give the county services a lot of credit because they had been extremely generous helping me get through the year of Sue's rehabilitation. I had no other choice at this time but to give the kids over to foster care. I didn't want to do this and I agonized over the decision. I had to do what was in their best interests. My life was crumbling before my eyes.

My brother in law and his wife stepped up and took the kids on a temporary basis. I released my kids to them and promised them that I would come back for them when I could pull things together. I signed the papers at a gas station.

I went to live with my uncle and worked during the week and would visit the kids each weekend. They were living in Connecticut at the time so it was an hour and a half trip for me. I was so grateful to my in laws for being there for my family. I was told by my mother and her attorney that I had better get a divorce in case my wife became a ward of the court. In that case I would be responsible for her and her expenses.

My mother arranged for me to get a Mexican divorce. I left New York in the Fall of 1968 and flew to El Paso, Texas. The next morning a limousine picked me up and took me across the border to Juarez and dropped me off, along with several others, on the steps of the court house.

When we got inside they told me to just nod my head when they called my name. I did that and then we left through the back door to the waiting limo. It was all very fast.

On the trip home I reflected on my life and felt like quite a failure. I was alone, divorced, with my relatives living far away and my kids in foster care. But I couldn't give up. I had the promise to my children to make happen. Life had to get better for me.

I took an apartment near work in Yonkers. It was in the rear of a private home and it had its own entrance. It was a small, one bedroom with a small kitchen and similar living rom. Best of all I could afford it at $100.00 a month. My now ex-wife took an apartment nearby, met someone else and got remarried. I was heartbroken. This marriage lasted only thirty days. I had no choice but to continue with my life and as time went on the pain lessened. I worked long hours at the store and had no time for women or dating.

My brother was home from the service and came to visit me. He was working for RCA at the time. One day we went to lunch at a nearby restaurant and ran into a friend of mine. She told us of a party to be held that night and invited us. We went to the party and met some girls there. My brother ended up marrying one of them. They fixed me up with a young girl named Jane, who was divorced and had two young sons aged 3 and 1. Upon introduction I thought she was gorgeous and I was attracted to her. We began dating and I later moved into her place. We were extremely compatible and I fell in love with her. She introduced me to her parents who seemed very nice. I was happy again. I had found someone to rescue.

Soon after I settled in with Jane, I was able to start my own appliance store in a town called Dobbs Ferry. I found a partner who put up $7000 Dollars. I was scared but I had always wanted my own business. So, I took the chance.

Nobody ever became successful without taking a gamble. Business was pretty good in the beginning. I was selling items fairly well. But after six or eight months my partner didn't want to continue funding me so I had to close the store. Needless to say I was heartbroken. My first real attempt at being self -employed was a bust. But someone once told me that the <u>key to success was through failure</u>.

With the store closed and me out of a job, the family decided to move to California where we both had family. My sister lived in Glendale at the time and Jane's parents lived in Arizona. We flew to Arizona, stayed with family through the Christmas holidays and then rented a car and drove to Glendale on January1, 1971. I arrived with 35 cents in my pocket. I had to find a job!

We found a house to rent. The owner was the nicest man. It had a small back house inhabited by a lady named Jean. After taking several small jobs, I was hired to work for an appliance store in the Valley. I had borrowed $700. from my father in law to buy a car. I bought a used VW bug with a new engine. It was hard having only one car, but we did it. Jane would take me to work and pick me up at 10:00 with the boys asleep in the back seat. I worked there for several months until I heard about an opening with a large appliance maker. I applied for a sales job. I was the first salesman ever hired without a college degree. They liked my experience with appliances and with the buying groups in the East. I was hired to take over a territory in the Los Angeles area. I was given a car allowance to cover expenses. It was $137.50 every two weeks. Part of my territory were the high desert towns of Palmdale and Lancaster. Driving a VW with no air conditioning was not fun especially during the summer months.

At the end of my first year with the company I was first in sales for my region and fourth in the country. Wow, what an accomplishment! I was given a trip to Marco Island, Florida as a reward. I was awarded a medal and the recognition of being in the top five salesmen in the entire country. I began to believe that if you obtain the recognition that the money and fame will follow.

Jane was pregnant with our daughter at the time of the trip. On the plane we met a regional manager whose wife was named Tiffany. Mt wife liked the name so much that we named our daughter Tiffany.

As time went on I continued to improve my sales and marketing skills. I started a company called The Egg-man. I found these guys who had a chicken ranch in San Diego. The concept was to sell them ranges that were in heavy demand and that the company could not keep in stock.

When a dealer called me for a particular model and color, and I made sure that The Egg-man had it in stock. The dealer would pick up the appliance and my guys would make twenty five to fifty dollars on the sale. It was a win-win for everyone. My volume continued to grow and I had all the eggs and chicken I wanted. I was on my way to great things.

My daughter was born and I loved her to death. She was so cute. I just wanted to work hard for my family and give them everything I never had.

I had my sights set on advancing in the company to a management position. I dreamed of Vice President. As time went on I began so see the politics of the corporate world unfold and it wasn't pretty. There was a regional manager position that I wanted really bad. Three of us were being considered for the position. In the end, they gave it to an outsider. One of the guys quit and became vice-president of a competing company. That made my job harder since he was now my competition.

Now that I had my career in full swing I had a promise to my children to fulfill. The kids were no longer living with their aunt and uncle but had been switched to another foster home. I contacted the children's services in New York and tried to get through all the red tape they presented.

They worked in conjunction with the Los Angeles offices and made home visits. Their big concern was that the kids would not be indigent. We had a nice house at the time and the visit went well. Still the New York offices would not release my kids to me. My lawyer told me that I was going to have to go back there and bring them back myself. Jane and I boarded a plane and went to visit the kids for a weekend. We took them with just the clothes on their backs and boarded the next plane to Los Angeles. I was so scared, constantly looking over my shoulder. When we landed I called the foster parents and told them that the kids were safe with me and they wouldn't be returning. I never heard another word from social services or anyone concerning this. I had promised my children that I would come for them and I did.

I had always wanted to be self-employed and I never lost sight of it. I began researching small companies with products that I could distribute in Southern California. I had been to an RV show at Dodger Stadium and I saw a small generator which interested me. I talked to the salesman about the product and found out the name of the company who built it. I called the factory and spoke to a sale manager. We spoke the same sales language and hit it off right away.

By the end of the conversation I had become the factory distributor for all of Southern California, Arizona, New Mexico, Nevada and Hawaii. It was a lot of work along with my main appliance job. I finally had to give up the areas of New Mexico and Arizona.

One of my accounts was a company called Bill's. The main salesman there was John and his friend Tom. These guys liked me and respected my opinion about the appliance business. They wanted to open their own business and wanted my input on good locations. I suggested an area where there were no other appliance stores. They took my advice and opened their store. It was a big success for them. They eventually opened several more stores. Their ego's got so big that they felt no one could bring them down. I was their hero. So, when I wanted to start my own company they agreed to back me. I opened Eagle Distributors and gave notice to company which had been my lifesaver. I hated to leave but having my own business was my dream, A retired vice president from the company agreed to come work for me to get the business started. I worked very hard to make a go of this company. I even hired my brother an another friend to help but I couldn't make enough to support a family and to employees. I had to go back to the appliance company and ask for my job back. Luckily they rehired me.

I continued selling the generators on the side. That business began to grow. I finally had to make a decision to once again quit the appliance company. I did it and never looked back.

I was shipping between 50 and 100 generators a month and doing very well. I remember buying my wife a new Corvette in 1982. I loved being able to provide extras for my family. I bought a small commercial building in our town. It was nice. It even had a downstairs which I made into a shop. I sold gas generators and put them on display on the first floor. The business grew and was profitable.

My family was getting used to having extra money to spend. My wife was spending so much money that I was losing control of her spending. Her boys were in middle school and getting into trouble. My wife didn't know how to handle them so she basically just closed her eyes on their behaviors. She couldn't handle the responsibility any more. The boys were seemingly out of control.

Eventually the boys were put into a mental health facility for youths where they would be safe and their problems could be worked on. I didn't agree with this decision but I had no legal say because I had never legally adopted them. This facility was like a prison with total lock down and no freedom to leave. They attended school at the facility. The boys began to smoke while they were there as well.

I remember that Jane had promised to bring them home for Thanksgiving. I got a call from the boys on Thanksgiving saying that mom had never come for them. I raced down there to pick them up to spend the day with them. The boys never forgave their mother for this.

Needless to say this took a toll on our marriage. The boys were eventually released but my wife couldn't handle things at home. She decided that she didn't want to be married anymore or be a mother. I was served divorce papers on Halloween 1982. Once again my life was falling apart.

I didn't know what to do. I left and went to my sister's house. The kids stayed with my wife.

I soon found out that she was seeing a young man who had been my daughter's friend. He had spent time at our house and eaten many dinners with us. Now he was fooling around with my wife. I think that she felt she could control him where she couldn't control me. I eventually hired a lawyer to handle the divorce. The divorce process was rough. Initially I was given custody of our youngest daughter, the only one under 18, but Tiffany later chose to be with her mother. I relinquished custody.

Jane moved six times during the first two years. I kept in touch with Tiffany as much as I could. She wasn't getting along with her mother but I had little control. Tiffany was beginning to drive and I wanted to buy her a vehicle so she could get around and visit me. I told her she would have to behave and keep going to school. She wanted a truck. We shopped around and found a black Nissan truck on the showroom floor. It was beautiful. Tiffany loved it. I paid cash for it and off we went. My daughter was so excited. And I was so happy that I could do this for her.

As time went by I found out that Tiffany was skipping school. I talked to her but she continued to skip classes. So, I drove to where she was living and took the truck and sold it to a friend the same day. I lost a lot of money on this but she needed to be taught a lesson. When she came home and found the truck gone she had a fit.

Tiffany eventually met a young man named Tom. She really liked him and moved in with him in their own apartment. She was 17 at the time. She went to court and got herself emancipated so she would be seen as an adult in the eyes of the courts. This meant that I could stop the child support payments. Although I didn't pay a lot, I resented sending money to help Jane and her boyfriend. Tiffany and Tom moved to Virginia to be near her brothers. This didn't last long and she soon called and asked to come home.

By this time my oldest daughter was working for the county courts and began dating a marshal named John. One day John came to me and asked for her hand in marriage. I had sort of been expecting this. I told him he had my blessing but if he ever physically hurt her I would take care of him. They married in 1992 and are still happily married. They have given me two beautiful grand children who I love very much.

After my second divorce I was very careful with dating. I was a middle aged man who still enjoyed the company of women but I would not be quick to jump into marriage. I joined a group for parents without partners. They held weekly dances which provided an opportunity to meet others who were in the same situation. I had many fun times at these dances and met a group of friends many of whom are still friends. The organization had a rule that you had to be a single parent but your spouse had to be alive. A nice lady who was widowed was denied membership in the group. Several of us didn't think that this was fair so we quit the group and started our own group. We held our own dances. Our membership grew and eventually the original group fell apart. These dances continued for 25 years. I had several girlfriends during this time. One relationship lasted several years.

My generator company was doing very well. One day I was reading something and got the idea for my next endeavor. I was already selling the small electric, generator. I could use it to provide stand-by power for the outpatient operating rooms. A law had recently been passed by the state that mandated emergency power be available during an operation where the patient is non ambulatory. I contacted local plastic surgeons an began installing my generators and invertors in doctor's offices. Not only did I do the installation, but doctors bought a monthly maintenance package to regularly service the system. The business of providing stand-by power for medical outpatient services grew very profitable. I had doctor clients all over California. Once a month I had to visit each office and service the system. I employed a person to help with this but I made sure to closely oversee each system. It was very time consuming but profitable.

By the early 1990's I had saved some money and decided to invest in real estate. I began looking at houses in the Valley. I finally found one on a cul de sac with a large lot. I rented my house in Sunland and moved into this new house. My girlfriend at the time, Mary, moved in with me.

Life was pretty good for a while. Mary and I did pretty well together. She was involved in several small businesses of her own and we traveled some. She was one of my partners in the dance business so our social life revolved around that. I bought my first motor home and we had fun traveling and meeting new friends. Mary's daughter came to live with us for a time before she got married.

I was feeling some discontent with the situation and eventually decided I needed to be alone. I told Mary that I wasn't happy and that we should split up. She took it well and moved out to be near her daughter. I have always questioned my decision. I know that she was the best friend I ever had. What confused me was that she never fought my decision or tried to discuss things. I cried a few tears over this. I had my house to myself and I was alone.

I desperately wanted someone in my life. I dated a lot of women but found no one who seemed right. One night in December of 2000, I was at the dance sitting near the entry when a lady came in who caught my eye. Her name was Nancy. We danced and danced that night. We began dating. I really felt that this was the one for me. However, after several months of dating I began to notice some strange behaviors. They are hard to describe here. We took a trip to Oregon with the motor home. We were in a little town at a restaurant and it was 80 degrees out. Nancy complained that she was cold. I suggested that she take my credit card and buy a sweatshirt. She came out of the shop with a fifty dollar blouse and no sweatshirt. I told her that this was an excessive charge and she became very angry. She went back to the store and bought the blouse on her card. When we got back to the coach she continued to be mad, I finally asked for the engagement ring back which I had just bought for her. She said that she wanted to go home. I made arrangements for her to fly home. I gave her $100.00 and said good-by. I felt terrible about this but no woman was going to give me grief like this. After she got home she called and wanted to come back and drive home with me. We stayed together for several more months as I continued to witness bizarre behavior. Nancy said that she wanted compensation to get married. She wanted one of my houses. I tried to ignore this kind of behavior but it wasn't easy. In July 2001, we were in Palm Springs when I suffered a heart attack. Nancy called the paramedics. I was taken to the local hospital where they put in a stint. I was. fixed up within an hour and doing fine. My relationship with Nancy continued to worsen. She left again and later returned. She even got me to go to therapy with her. Finally I said that I had taken enough. The parting didn't go smoothly but I finally got her out of my life. I don't know why I put up with so much. I did love her but her issues were more than I could handle.

I continued to date women of interest but no one seemed just right. I joined a dating organization called Great Expectations to widen the scope of possibilities. Before the days of the internet, this company took videos of individuals and the individuals submitted a short biography. Members would come in and search books of biographies and find possible matches. One day I got a phone call from the company indicating a lady had requested interest in me. I contacted her and set a date for dinner at a local restaurant. She is a retired elementary school principal and a widow of three years. Her pictures look good. I hope that this works out for me.

We went on our date which I fondly call the date from hell. Her name is Judy. She entered the restaurant looking good but very cautious. We sat down in a curved booth but she chose to sit opposite me. I asked her to move closer but she indicated that she was fine where she was. After the meal I walked her to her car which was a distance from the restaurant. She got in and drove off. She never even asked if she could drive me to my car. I waited almost a week to call her. I asked her to go on a picnic with me. We went to the store and bought the fixings for sandwiches and then went to the marina. She didn't know that I had a boat there. We had a great time and she enjoyed the boat. We continued to date and we enjoyed each other. After several months I decided to buy another motor home. I found one in Tampa, Florida and made all arrangements over the phone. We flew down to Florida the day after Christmas, picked up the coach and drove it back to Los Angeles. We had a great time and met some wonderful people along the way.

We took quite a few trips with the motor home and attended several rallies. Judy really enjoyed the motor home life. She had never been exposed to it before. During the summer we visited some friends in McKenzie Bridge, Oregon. They have a lot in a private motor home park. We had such a good time visiting them. We looked into possibly purchasing a lot for our coach. I found the lot I wanted but it wasn't available at the time. Several months later I was offered the lot and I bought it. We improved the lot and spent over 10 years of summer months enjoying friends and the area of McKenzie Bridge.

During the following years I began having back troubles. I had to have several major back surgeries within a three year period. Each one was successful but my back had so much damage that it never healed without pain. My back got so bad that I couldn't drive my motor home any more.

I had to hire a driver to bring it home for me from Oregon. I eventually turned it back to the bank on a voluntary repossession. It just didn't make sense to keep something that expensive when I couldn't use it. It was a very sad day for both of us.

Eventually my back got a little better and we missed the motor home and our friends. Judy decided to buy a smaller coach that she could drive. For a couple of years it worked pretty well. We would trade off driving every two hours and never drive over five hours a day.

I seems that once I hit my 70's my body decided to give up on life. Not only did I have to contend with the pain from my back, but in 2013 I was diagnosed with bladder cancer. The initial diagnosis was made in Oregon. Tests were done and it was determined that the tumor had not gone beyond the bladder wall. We had a follow up appointment to begin treatment with doctors at USC and they said that it had penetrated the wall. This meant that the best treatment was surgery and removal of the bladder. They said that without surgery I wouldn't live two years.

I was not up for another surgery. I am slow to recover from any surgery and at the age of 72 I didn't want to spend whatever time was left in a recovery mode. I found an oncologist who believed in chemo and radiation treatment.

I had two chemo sessions and 36 sessions of radiation. That was five years ago and I am now cancer free. Two years ago I was diagnosed with COPD and was put on oxygen. This is a result of years of smoking. Even though I had quit almost 40 years ago, the damage done to my lungs caught up with me. A year later they found a spot on my right breast which was malignant. I had mastectomy. At the moment I am cancer free and maintaining a pretty good quality of life. I treat every day as an adventure never knowing what new issue may appear.

I had the opportunity to sell both of my businesses to the same person. I took advantage of this and tried to retire. I found it very difficult to do nothing. My interests are few and I missed the thrill of a sales call and closing a deal. I found a small product related to my motorhome interest and began selling it. I was pretty busy during the first few years but now sales have slowed. Maybe it is because I have slowed down.

At this point I am very comfortable with my life. As I reflect back I realize how hard I worked to get to this point. I had to overcome a lot of obstacles along the way. There were many times when I could have given up but then I would have lost everything I had. I had to persevere and keep my long term goals in sight. Too many people were depending on me. I started my life with few material advantages but through hard work, perseverance, and a strong sense of responsibility I amassed a very comfortable life. I have children doing well with their own families, four beautiful grandchildren, a roof over my head and a good woman by my side.

I have written this accounting of my life primarily for my children and grandchildren and for their descendants yet to come. I want them to know about me, their heritage, and maybe learn from some of my decisions.

Printed in the United States
By Bookmasters